I0210421

Orchard Language

poems by

Kathy Pon

Finishing Line Press
Georgetown, Kentucky

Orchard Language

"The grower of trees, the gardener, the man born to farming
Whose hands reach into the ground and sprout
To him the soil is a divine drug."
        —Wendell Berry, *The Man Born to Farming*

Copyright © 2025 by Kathy Pon
ISBN 979-8-89990-187-4 First Edition
All rights reserved under International and Pan-American Copyright Conventions.
No part of this book may be reproduced in any manner whatsoever without written
permission from the publisher, except in the case of brief quotations embodied in
critical articles and reviews.

ACKNOWLEDGMENTS

The author would like to thank the editors of the following journals in which
these poems first appeared:

Canary: "Neighborhood Dwelling"
Dionysian Public Library "*Propagate*" Anthology: "Orchard Language"
Eunoia Review: "Wintering"
Flora Fiction Literary Magazine: "Unresolved"
Gilded Weathervane Journal: "Pothole Anthem"
Passengers Journal: "Preservation"
Plants and Poetry Journal: "Tomato Farmer"
The Avenue Journal: "Dam Ambition"
The Orchards Poetry Journal: "Clockwork"
The Tiger Moth Review: "Enough"

Publisher: Leah Huete de Maines
Editor: Christen Kincaid
Cover Art: Julie Collins
Author Photo: Terri Sorensen
Cover Design: Elizabeth Maines McCleavy

Order online: www.finishinglinepress.com
also available on amazon.com

Author inquiries and mail orders:
Finishing Line Press
PO Box 1626
Georgetown, Kentucky 40324
USA

Table of Contents

Neighborhood Dwelling

We, the only humans for fifty acres,
a three-sixty surround-screen
of brown and green. From any window,
our tree-neighbors can be seen.
Their limbs lift skyward
celebrating this year's water allocation,
worshiping a gracious sun.

Not streets but rows. Where inhabitants
amplify each season, delirious décor
filling the senses. Bloom's perfume,
full leaf's foliage. Nuts raining down
at harvest, dormancy's hush.
Years, we follow their growth,
tiny saplings to prolific producers
as if we were watching kids
down the block mature.

Husband and I form the ultimate
Neighborhood Watch, four-wheeling
with valve fittings and knives.
Farm aid repairing geysers
from each coyote-chewed dripline.
Vigilant, we scan berms
for weeds, assess color of leaves,
the nuances of well-being.
Probing soil for moisture, we rub
samples between fingers and thumb.
Check for hull split and orange worm,
pests boring their way into nuts.

And as we tend to this orchard,
we ourselves are tended.
Each tree's green-gloved fingers quiver
in the breeze linking us to earth.

Tunnels of foliage slotted with sunbeams
beckon us to walk, our feet grounded
in the calm found beneath
a shady canopy. From any spot
symmetry in tree-trunk lines
rise before our eyes. In this space
we take cleansing breaths,
imagine the invisible
work of each tree scrubbing carbon
from the air, supplying
oxygen to the planet.

Our bodies move with farmland's
soundscape of crows and jays
and hawks perched atop
the highest boughs. Shrieks and screeches,
rural fowl speeches reverberate.
We find belief in the buzz of bees,
faith in the jingle of daytime cricket song.

Neither wilderness space
nor manicured yard,
but an almond orchard neighborhood
whose permanent residents invite our presence

to witness their vertical revelry
like a prayer surging skyward.
We are here. You are home.

Sheepherder Whistle

This ranch holds a spirit.

Your grandfather traded
mountain for valley.

At ninety his brittle bones,
defiant to time, whistled,

turning a perfect somersault
on barefoot-soft lawn.

A lamb frolics
after tasting orchardgrass.

      Who gets a chance to sing his body?

Not his son or the novena
of nine children cultivating

faith in Santa Clara's holy trinity:
apricots, prunes and cherries.

Growers humbled even as
blossoms became buildings.

      Husband, which way will you tumble?

Rooted now in the Central Valley,
you still hear his summons.

A herder's whistle stirs
your hungry heart.

Orchard Language I

Orchard language is thick,
with bloodline, sticking to
the tip of a longing tongue. It clings
in legacy, the cultivation of
soil, seedlings that pleat acres
staked with white cartons.

Before we marry, I meet
your mother, Machi. I realize
her first language is not Basque,
but farming. I hear in her voice
a cadence of the ranch
that nurtured you, fruit trees calling
your family to raise up agriculture
like a host to their lips.

We mortgage our safe suburban
beginnings for dirt of our own,
plant an almond orchard.
Immerse ourselves
in the linguistics of growers.

Tomato Farmer

Not a celebrated gardener.
No hoisted heirlooms or titan beefsteaks.
Husband, you till knowledge
a whole red industry in numbers.
How they spew from your mouth:
60-inch single beds
N 6428 varieties, 578 trays
$105 a ton, 375 million acre feet.

You can't pass a field
without audit. Squint,
assess each sprawling acre
sea of earth, tangled vines and fruit.
Your eyes detect the withered, wilt, rot.
Diseases dance on your lips: verticillium, thrips.
Afflictions like the common cold
roll in recital: blight, powdery mildew.
You lather remedies
like summer suntan lotions.
Apply this pre-emergent, spray that fungicide.

Still, I've learned to listen
to the silence,
and your quickened heartbeat
when you behold a fertile field
heavy in tonnage, glossy with health.
To feel your awe, thick as summer grass.

I wait for a sigh
your nod to the mighty tomato.

Pothole Anthem

We fly, high speed
crushing crumbled craters
pocking our path. Defy
disintegration, ignore the heft
of tractors, dairy trucks
chipping base rock and pitch.
Road residue, the honored
car sticker of backcountry roots.

Our kids race against
low-flying crop dusters
on their drive to school.
Car thumping gravel and dust,
jostling bodies and books.
Small town accelerated learning,
to navigate the asphalt minefield
and its daily demand for rubber.

After rain, tires smash
the cracks, spitting stones
and silt. Each jutted crevice
punches the truck, tears at tread,
wear out shocks and struts.
Broken, never-ending
rock-blasts, a road resolved
to return to earth.

Here we say
potholes are portals
to solid grounding.
Each trip a chance
to conquer the grueling
rural grind

Enough

Even on rural roads light obscures
dark skies. Stars strive to break through
an opaque vault. A nearby dairy's LEDs

stream, beaming rural enterprise.
Manure gleams like midnight jewels
beneath lumens burning bright in barns,

swelling cow teats, darkness shaved
to stimulate production. Head back,
I search skies remembering backcountry

nights, swirling light arching across
the universe. Now a shroud curtains
all but a few celestial bodies. Ursa Major

penetrates dust and glare, her brightest
stars cracking earth's bleached dome.
I plead for starlight traversing space,

astral beacons of wanderers and wisemen,
needing only darkness to illuminate.
All our best intentions light the night

yet dim the stars to glints in a haze
of our planet's glow. Will we forget
how to stargaze, our children unable

to trace the lucent spume of the Milky Way?

Wilting

I step into my yard to steal
what's left—delicious sips of August.
Final days trickle like molasses,
thick in finish. Peach leaves sputter,
spinning pirouettes in freefall.
Crimson zinnia corollas crisp
to shimmering copper cups
while snapdragon tips toast,
begging to be deadheaded.
My marigolds spill seeds,
savory like pepper, distracting Time,
her mouth open, ready to swallow
the season. Even beyond
this stucco wall, corn tassels dip,
heavy in the hot sun, thirsting
for harvest's relief.
On cue, dragonflies fill fields,
tokens of waning joy. Gossamer
wings whir and blur in flight,
swirling dives and climbs as if
kissed by molecules of air.

Are we, too, like August, floating
in envelopes of marriage swelter?
I am wilting, a flower in need of
tender gestures. To be gathered
in your hands, to feel fingertips
caress my neck. You lean long
towards cool, quiet spaces. Stretch
your body, soak up the sheltering
shade in a season of frenzied play.
Can we reach for summer's silk
threads, balloon across these long
days of light, evade fading
desire, our petals melting
in blades of grass?

Orchard Language II

Orchard language is lush
with leafy green unfurling
afternoon's light spray
stretched long
on the treeline. It speaks
in lilting branches, birdsong cascading
from canopy foliage, dragonflies
droning daylight.

By listening, I absorb vocabulary
of farming. In raindrops grazing
leaves, soaking deep into terrain,
I understand *aquifer*.
In the silent snore of dormancy
building towards bloom,
I comprehend *chill hours*.
I recognize groans of fullness,
almonds splitting leathery hulls
as *harvest*. I pronounce time
to *shake*, marveling in the soundscape
of drumming nuts falling to earth.

To orchard is to breathe life
into our almond seedlings.
Feed the soil, entreat
the sun and water to transform
their energy to nuts. Nurture them
like our own children.

Duck Season

Dawn marbles
the Pacific Flyway.
Shadows sharpen to shapes.
Willow, cattails jut from water
—and hunters
under cover, motionless. Tracking
lift, northern pintails, green winged teal,
bands of mallards cloaked in marsh reeds.
A rasp of duck calls charge
morning air, luring waterfowl
to sighting.

Gunshots pop and roll across the wetlands
—reverberating into my bedroom window.

We share the same sanctuary.
Birds stop for a stay
in their thousand-mile exodus,
revel in a habitat flush with food.
Hunters rise to nature's challenge,
christened in tradition
of dogs, guns, duck blinds.

Huntsmen and women observe
bag limits and three-day shooting weeks,
elevate duck to holiness
in gourmet recipes,
back conservation work
for this wintering habitat, a trade-off
I turn over in my mind,
each side bearing weight.

Still, as the season's first shells
thunder in the distance, I can only
search my own heart

too heavy to appreciate
how a shoveler breaks from its flock
in the mist, finishes
with a decisive shot.

Turkey Vultures

Roaming a remote stretch of canal
footsteps and breeze fill the air
as turkey vultures kettle above.
Scalloped silver-white wings
catch thermals, rising like drones
over farmland.

They descend, dark shadows
on an adjacent field, gather in wake,
feast on the flesh of a dead calf.
Hooked beaks like sickles tear
at the carcass.

Each bald red head pokes
into caverns of carrion, fearless.
Featherless faces
peck at entrails, sip the slick of blood,
devour gristle, pick at bones.

Tomorrow they huddle
in shredded bark branches
of a Blue Eucalyptus.
Sunlight invites takeoff,
a call to follow scent, fresh corpses.

Iron stomachs revel in rot,
digest putrefied flesh,
a cleaning crew clearing
the countryside of its dead.

Driven to eclipse the mess of decay,
raise death to banquet.

Preservation

You stash garbage bags and plastic gloves
in your trunk should you stumble
upon a rabbit or coyote killed
in a car collision.
Depending on time of death
you will pack the carcass
in the school staffroom freezer
for later transport.
Sometimes you must get a gorgeous
but not-so-fresh roadkill
to the taxidermist
and report yourself late to work.

Your house, filled with preserved creatures.
The Cooper's Hawk, wings posed in flight.
A black masked raccoon, paws raised
in attack. Even your late kitty,
tail vertical, ready to saddle up to your side.

Some say beasts should return to earth
in death. I love how you give them honor
reanimating their bodies.

I rent a place in town, you bring me
Gladys, a wheat-colored hen.
My guardian, you insist. Poised to strut,
feathers fluffed, wings lifted in rebuke.
Gladys' glass eyes stare me down
like an evil warden.

I happily return your fowl friend
when I move, still touched
by your largesse.

Parkinson's progresses, you decide
to move to Oregon to be near your daughter.
Your light dims with miles and time
—and deterioration
of nerve cells. Slowly,
I lose you

but still smile remembering
those mounted critters, imagine
even you might laugh
at the absurdity—

preservation of dead animals,
easier than keeping friendship alive.

Aging

We stand before our almond orchard,
trees clawed from earth, piled
in woody carnage.
Decline has prompted removal.

Now, chippers devour corpses,
spitting out organic material,
mulch to nurture the next seedlings.

I try to lean into
this *circle of life* idea

wondering about my own
arc of productivity.
I will be the withered one
when the next almond trees mature.

Unresolved

We have circled this orchard on foot
thousands of times, its borders
frayed, dirt ground to powder,
seeking rhythm.

How can we know what is true
when all around
earth and its creatures sigh
in equal parts—revolt and mercy?
Fighting decline, pleading
a different way.

I can only look for constants
of this farmland.

Skeins of Ibis forming
in morning sky toward irrigated pastures.

An egret's lift, low croak with slow
wingspan gracing the irrigation canal.

Always, sparrows and phoebes lighting
tops of branches like tiny stars,
a chorus chirping faith in timeless
weeds and seeds and daylight.

Still, uncertainty lodges in my hips,
muscles unwilling to flex with sunrise.

Today, every tree wilts, thick with
the resignation that comes from emptying.
Below, a cover crop of crisped safflower
practices how to come undone.
Don't we all taste rot at times
in our search for nourishment?

I glance at you in careful stride
beside me, conversation
dissipates in wisps of *shoulds* and *maybes*
or arbitrary agendas for the day because
we forget the language for desire.

I have become gray and weathered
like the bark of these trees
pushing through
disquiet,
sensing a pathway
right as rain.

Driving Somewhere Outside My Comfort Zone

I've not been this way in awhile. For miles
defoliated cotton flashes its flocked bolls,

wind swirls across the highway coughing
distrust. Banners on old farm trailers assail

Democrats for lost water. How I long to stop
and argue rain. American flags whip wildly

as if *We, the people* wish to fight. Further on,
signs proclaim *God! Family! Country!*

With no faith in church, frequent questions
of family and country—I am a sinner

in this place of devotion's hard-liners
and decrees, unfit for patriotic duty.

Hands at ten and two o'clock cramp in angst
with locals' rancor. Something they've lost—

a bird, now flown? Decades ago, I taught
farmworkers' kids here. Even then, scales

tipped towards landowners, a counterbalance
to *literacy for all.* Surely, I failed my students

in a system designed to reward the chosen.
I flush the shame of an outsider, can only focus

on the orchards. Nuts windrowed, mounded,
stony truths waiting to be swept.

This Valley's Legs Wobble

Soil's dry mouth
smacks, craving relief.
Until record storms deliver

rain. Liquid finds
permeable spaces, fills
earth's empty tissues.

Ground water restores
balance, hydrates cells
like a wellspring,

feeds roots & limbs,
rejuvenating terrain's
salt-dried epidermis.

Saturated, reservoirs
stretch like muscles
after a long drink.

Replenishment glorifies
withered sinew. I want to
believe in resurrection

yet aquifers sucked
dry do not rise. Dust
weighs on bones of land

where earth's lungs
have collapsed, where
wells once pumped

blood from this
desert-body. Health,
merely a mirage.

Dam Ambition

"...and all because there's water in one place and there isn't in another. "
    —JFK, San Luis Dam, 1962

Our towering San Luis earth-wall stores
snowmelt of the blue and wild, dammed

Delta watershed, diverted and pumped to
irrigate crops and quench the region's

thirst. We praise the visionary dam, forget
faith in coursing rivers, reciting a litany

of benefits to the valley: Desert greened
for more food, hydropower, flood control.

State and federal bureaucrats divide
and deliver this water like gods gifting

life to mortals in concrete arterials, canals
and aqueduct snaking the state for miles.

We swallow rivers, make an arid valley
fertile. This is our power. Still our ingenuity

confuses nature. Water temperatures rise,
salmon lose their way, and tule reeds

no longer lush shorelines. Debate rages
about benefits of dams until severe drought.

Then in uproar, angry voices demand more
storage. Here, people speak of earthquake

stability, water allocation, how to increase
capacity. Yet we never shift from our hubris—

we can solve big problems by squeezing
rivers, by altering land. Even as watermark

leaves its stain, as aquifer bones crumble.
As a stony sun scorches our tongues.

Clockwork

More than coffee, what gets me going: Ribbons
of white-faced ibis, noiseless, unfolding with sunrise.

V formation, vectors vibrant against a canvas
smeared pink, expanding to black cables, waltz

in flight. One undulation in unison, wings
flap and glide, necks extend forward, purposed.

How mysterious! Rhythms stirring trajectory,
magical hour of beetles and grasshoppers

crawling irrigated pastures. Quick drop,
long legs wade the mud-drenched fields,

curved bills probe downward. Indigo foragers
busy beneath a warming sun. Ignoring me

as I stroll by, a whole congregation absorbed in
fowl activities. Later, at dusk, a bookending of day,

ibis again lift, inky lines reshape to Victory,
home bound to roost, nests in sedgy grasses.

Perfection, these circadian sky-time sweeps,
a wild avian faithfulness to each moment.

Call to Winter

Under a silvery sky
slim leaf stems grasp branches
before breaking
into tired butterflies. Floating
     freely on whorls of air
        earthward
to blanket our orchard floor, yellow
praise to the season.

We walk in silence,
chill shakes our bones, hands
dig further into pockets, fingering
a memory of heat seamed
in darkness. Collars up,
our faces windshield first raindrops
tap-tapping an impending storm.

What a perfect morning to stack
almond wood, those crusty old men
crowded in cords behind the shop.
Drag out the steel log rack
your brother welded last Christmas
before we understood
stage four.
Just for a moment
caress the indomitable iron
left to fill our longing hearth.

We wheelbarrow piles of cured logs
to the covered porch,
layer them like brown jelly rolls.
Splendid sustenance ready
like us, to burn brightly
despite muted trees, earth's tilt away
from sunlight. Trusting

our inner clock,
attentive to a call to winter.

Wintering

quiet invites quiet
—what follows a gasp of wonder
at smeared stars across an inked galaxy
a forest, muted after fallen snow
tranquil as a child's prayer

yield to winter
your slackened muscles resist
filling every droplet of time
with go go go

cold disables internal clamor
invites cerebration

lean into laying low
a loosened schedule
curl of breath on a chilly day
fog's milky dream
where thought lingers
self breathes clutter out of self
acuity returns

wintering, a regenerative balm
on your withered heart

in this embrace of slow motion
a hushed version of you
whispers strength
like bare root trees
dormant, waiting

Pruning Master

Jacket zipped against winter fog,
warm breath rising,
you stride to the shop. Emerge
with loppers and shears, drop
them on the dormant ground.
Begin your study
of each bare fruit tree,
awaiting spring.

First, the big trimmer. Fat blades
for thick branches shading each other.
I notice a pondering before
each chop, stringing into cadence:
Pause, then lop. Pause, then lop.
Branches topple to ground
in bristled percussion
while bird chitter rises, thin
notes piping.
Key of spare, elegance
filling my own limbs.

Skilled sculpturer, you open
each tree to its core, window
to the sun, the promise for
vigorous growth.

Orchard Language III

Orchard is my second language.
I still struggle to explain
branch-chatter, how owls jewel
evening treetops, the spirits
spinning yellowed leaves
into butterflies before they blanket
the orchard floor. Yet I spout
water needs from my mouth,
estimating 150-acre feet.
Eloquence springs forth
as kinship deepens
with this land.

I learn to utter *sustainable*
like a blessing, lips parted back,
breath pushing past my teeth,
reassurance released into the orchard,
word becomes a way of life.

Before she passes, I catch Machi
smiling, pleased with my fluency
in her mother tongue.

Faithful

Husband composes his mother's eulogy,
memories of a tender shepherdess unfold

as I walk the orchard in January stumble,
searching for signs, a guiding talisman.

I sight your teardrop shape from berms
of mud. Tail feathers, crown, brilliant white

announce your migratory return. To anoint
shoots in hardpan, branches in budswell.

From afar you prophet, fixed head crooked,
shepherd's staff atop walnut tree. Talons bless

what we can't understand. Like praise you lift,
plumage inks sky with belief, soaring stitches

heaven to earth. Loss caught in eagle's flight,
aerial surrender to the endless ache.

We Give Our Backroad Away

These jagged chips, cracks
like open wounds. Can I withstand
more jarring jolts, endless
flat tires? I'm fatigued, shoulders stiff
from bracing bumps. *Can we just
get this dirt road paved?* I need
a disciplined drive, potholes filled,
dust and gravel swallowed.
A slick silver path, yellow dashes
cleanly separating two sides.
I need an uneventful to-and-from.
You shake your head. *Be careful
what you wish for.*

We give our backroad away.

Farmland reverberates with
earth movers, then surrenders
to loaded tomato rigs barreling past,
a short-cut to canneries.
Perhaps drivers appreciate this smooth
two-mile stretch of pristine county
road flanked by almond orchard and dairy.
Maybe they hear the soil sigh
when tires swish past.
Or they mock the county for wasting
their slick thoroughfare on
three undeserving homeowners.

One afternoon after the usual
long-distance grocery run to town
I snap, *Geez! I forgot the coffee!*
Your smile pacifies
before your truck peels away
on a dustless horizon.

I sit on the porch to wait.
Does cushy asphalt soothe
inconvenience? Or does pavement prove
we've let our ancestors down,
forgotten husbandry for the land,
caved to urban comfort?

Between branches, a black cement ribbon
flashes in both directions.
I ask the trees for forgiveness.

February Rescue

Morning sky, a shiny silver fish crested
by rainbow. Water-colored light halos
soggy hills to my west. Mist is forming
over the endless muck, muddied road
crusted from two days of wind. Stoic
almond trees mark time with budswell
forming on a few bare limbs. Unlikely
a groundhog here will catch its shadow.

> I walk along, both dogs nosing earth's
> rot, dirty paws excavating gopher holes.
> Wind blasts send my icy hands deeper
> into down pockets. Slop and shivers
> make me wish for warmer days, buds
> opening, paper-thin petals exploding
> in sunshine. Perfumed breezes casting
> a spell upon me. All I want is spring.

But I must wait. A sunny day will arrive,
then step out. Hear wingbeat music of bees,
nature's fairies footprinting each blossom,
dusting flowers to nutlets. Bless creatures
bringing passage to renewed life. As if a
prelude, white boxes now dot the treeline,
stacked and staggered in eights. Spring's
dance partners queued for a bloom ball.

> I run like a child finding packages
> of promise delivering orchard magic.
> The ageless gift, winter cracked open
> eases a restlessness growling within.
> I shortcut through the trees. Both dogs
> yelp, hackles up, daring to creep closer.
> Whistle them back. Not farm equipment
> but better—the beehives have arrived.

Practicing Resurrection

We stop at the Quick Mart on Highway 33
between the surfboard laundromat
and tax accountant. An outpost
conveniently located for lifestyle changes,
canvassed in twelve-pack beer bargains
for drive-by winners.
You buy a Lotto ticket. We could use
a little jackpot

after our odyssey with the overly helpful
insurance lady navigating us through
Medicare's maze of care packages.
On the drive home, we add up each part
like a bill on some swanky cruise.

Sixty-fifth summer. Each day a chance
to practice resurrection. Your hair, streaked
silver, my skin, antique bronze.
Faithful bodies rise
to activity, stay in motion. Ignore
stiff joints. Shamelessly crave
cocktails. Creep closer to
selling the ranch.

Sometimes we sleepwalk
through each other's unfinished dreams
scanning for clues,
a map to the next destination.

I write poetry, you stream
zany *YouTube* videos. We hallway-meet
to plan dog walks and dinner.
Urgency still hits. I cannot permit
this afternoon to vaporize. C'mon, let's pull out
that new turntable, find classics. Turn up
the volume, rock out
like it's nineteen eighty-six.

Black Walnut Tree on the Irrigation Canal

Her prominence. Her eminence
presides over the waterway
and queendom of loamy graded farmground.
Shading, serenading crows, her rustling
leaves shimmy in the breeze.
While her crown offers peace
to one sandhill crane.
Boughs outstretched, her majesty
reflected upside-down in the water,
extolls the oddities of grit.

The nearby stolen pickup
abandoned on the canal,
how surrender white-washes
bad habits. Or fresh manure beyond,
shredded and spread like brown rain
on forage, a plan to mitigate leaching.
Across in a field, farmworkers
harvest tomatoes, their dreams
of citizenship pressed against
the weight of daily bad press.
And each day, a fisherman,
afternoon stop. Trunk open,
line cast, a quick chance to catch
an aqueduct carp. Pickle
its bones for the children.

Empress of all trees shakes
her stately branches. I know
she possesses secrets of resiliency
in this beautiful, wounded place. I lean in
to listen, my assumptions wrought
with blame and fault. Must I cut off
my ears to silence the noise?
She remains stoic, unfazed
by the strange, her tenacious gray trunk
praises the profane.

Kathy Pon earned a doctorate in education, but in retirement has returned to her life-long passion for reading and writing poetry. Her husband is a third-generation farmer, and they live in the middle of a Central California almond orchard with their two dogs. She is a member of two monthly poetry groups, is an avid pickleball player, and enjoys hiking and swimming.

Her work has been published in *Wildroof Journal, Passengers Journal, Canary, RockPaperPoem, The Tiger Moth Review, The Closed Eye Op*en and other places. Her chapbook, *Orchard Language* (Finishing Line Press) is published in 2025. Find her at *kathleenpon@gmail.com.*

www.ingramcontent.com/pod-product-compliance
Lightning Source LLC
Chambersburg PA
CBHW022053080426
42734CB00009B/1320